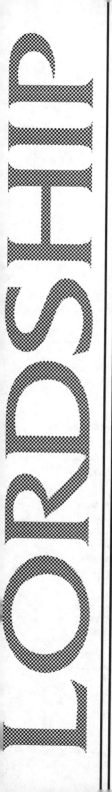

LORDSHIP

Basic Disciple-ship

FLOYD M^cCLUNG

WITH DALE & SANDY LARSEN

**6 studies
for individuals or groups**

CHRISTIAN BASICS BIBLE STUDIES

With Guidelines for
Leaders & Study Notes
NIV Text Included

InterVarsity Press
Downers Grove, Illinois, USA
Leicester, England

‖‖‖‖‖ W9-AHM-744

InterVarsity Press
P.O. Box 1400, Downers Grove, IL 60515, USA
38 De Montfort Street, Leicester LE1 7GP, England

©1996 by Floyd McClung

*All rights reserved. No part of this book may be reproduced in any form without written permission
from InterVarsity Press, P.O. Box 1400, Downers Grove, IL 60515.*

*InterVarsity Press® is the book-publishing division of InterVarsity Christian Fellowship®, a student
movement active on campus at hundreds of universities, colleges and schools of nursing in the
United States of America, and a member movement of the International Fellowship of Evangelical
Students. For information about local and regional activities, write Public Relations Dept.,
InterVarsity Christian Fellowship, 6400 Schroeder Rd., P.O. Box 7895, Madison, WI 53707-7895.*

*All Scripture quotations, unless otherwise indicated, are taken from the HOLY BIBLE, NEW
INTERNATIONAL VERSION®. NIV®. Copyright ©1973, 1978, 1984 by International Bible Society.
Used by permission of Zondervan Publishing House. All rights reserved.*

This study guide is based on and adapts material from Basic Discipleship ©1988, 1990 by Floyd
McClung, *published originally under the title* Wholehearted *and used with permission of Harper
Collins Publishers Limited, London.*

*Inter-Varsity Press, England, is the book-publishing division of the Universities and Colleges
Christian Fellowship (formerly the Inter-Varsity Fellowship), a student movement linking
Christian Unions in universities and colleges throughout the United Kingdom and the Republic of
Ireland, and a member movement of the International Fellowship of Evangelical Students. For
information about local and national activities write to UCCF, 38 De Montfort Street, Leicester
LE1 7GP.*

Cover photograph: Michael Goss

Cover background: Cowgirl Stock Photography ©1991

USA ISBN 0-8308-2015-9
UK ISBN 0-85111-378-8

Printed in the United States of America ♾

| 20 | 19 | 18 | 17 | 16 | 15 | 14 | 13 | 12 | 11 | 10 | 9 | 8 | 7 | 6 | 5 | 4 | 3 | 2 | 1 |

| 12 | 11 | 10 | 09 | 08 | 07 | 06 | 05 | 04 | 03 | 02 | 01 | 00 | 99 | 98 | 97 | 96 |

Getting the Most Out of Christian Basics Bible Studies

Knowing Christ is where faith begins. From there we grow through the essentials of discipleship: Bible study, prayer, worship, Christian community and much more. We learn to set godly priorities, overcome spiritual opposition and witness to others. These are the topics woven into each of the Christian Basics Bible Studies. Working through this series will help you become a more mature Christian.

What Kind of Guide Is This?

The studies are not designed to merely tell you what one person thinks. Instead, through inductive study, they will help you discover for yourself what Scripture is saying. Each study deals with a particular passage—rather than jumping around the Bible—so that you can really delve into the author's meaning in that context.

The studies ask three different kinds of questions. *Observation* questions help you to understand the content of the passage by asking about the basic facts: who, what, when, where and how. *Interpretation* questions delve into the meaning of the passage. *Application* questions help you discover its implications for growing in Christ. These three keys unlock the treasures of the biblical writings and help you live them out.

This is a thought-provoking guide. Each question assumes a variety of answers. Many questions do not have "right" answers, particularly questions that aim at meaning or application. Instead, the questions should inspire users to explore the passage more thoroughly.

This study guide is flexible. You can use it for individual study, but it is also great for a variety of groups—student, professional, neighborhood or church groups. Each study takes about forty-five minutes in a group setting or thirty minutes in personal study.

How They're Put Together
Each study is composed of four sections: opening paragraphs and questions to help you get into the topic, the NIV text and questions that invite study of the passage, questions to help you apply what you have learned, and a suggestion for prayer.

The workbook format provides space for writing a response to each question. This format is ideal for personal study and allows group members to prepare in advance for the discussion and/or write down notes during the study. This space can form a permanent record of your thoughts and spiritual progress.

At the back of the guide are study notes which may be useful for leaders or for individuals. These notes do not give "the answers," but they do provide additional background information on certain questions to help you through the difficult spots. The

"Guidelines for Leaders" section describes how to lead a group discussion, gives helpful tips on group dynamics and suggests ways to deal with problems which may arise during the discussion. With such helps, someone with little or no experience can lead an effective group study.

Suggestions for Individual Study

1. If you have not read the book or booklet suggested in the "further reading" section, you may want to read the portion suggested before you begin your study.

2. Read the introduction. Consider the opening questions and note your responses.

3. Pray, asking God to speak to you from his Word about this particular topic.

4. Read the passage reproduced for you in the New International Version. You may wish to mark phrases that seem important. Note in the margin any questions that come to your mind as you read.

5. Use the questions from the study guide to more thoroughly examine the passage. Note your findings in the space provided. After you have made your own notes, read the corresponding study notes in the back of the book for further insights.

6. Reread the entire passage, making further notes about its general principles and about the way you intend to use them.

7. Move to the "commit" section. Spend time prayerfully considering what the passage has to say specifically to your life.

8. Read the suggestion for prayer. Speak to God about insights you have gained. Tell him of any desires you have for specific growth. Ask him to help you as you attempt to live out the principles described in that passage.

Suggestions for Members of a Group Study

Joining a Bible study group can be a great avenue to spiritual growth. Here are a few guidelines that will help you as you participate in the studies in this guide.

1. These studies focus on a particular passage of Scripture— in depth. Only rarely should you refer to other portions of the Bible, and then only at the request of the leader. Of course, the Bible is internally consistent. Other good forms of study draw on that consistency, but inductive Bible study sticks with a single passage and works on it in depth.

2. These are discussion studies. Questions in this guide aim at helping a group discuss together a passage of Scripture in order to understand its content, meaning and implications. Most people are either natural talkers or natural listeners. Yet this type of study works best if people participate more or less evenly. Try to curb any natural tendency to either excessive talking or excessive quiet. You and the rest of the group will benefit.

3. Most questions in this guide allow for a variety of answers. If you disagree with someone else's comment, gently say so. Then explain your own point of view from the passage before you.

4. Be willing to lead a discussion, if asked. Much of the preparation for leading has already been accomplished in the writing of this guide.

5. Respect the privacy of people in your group. Many people speak of things within the context of a Bible study/prayer group that they do not want to be public knowledge. Assume that personal information spoken within the group setting is private, unless you are specifically told otherwise. And don't talk about it elsewhere.

6. We recommend that all groups follow a few basic guidelines and that these guidelines be read at the first session. The guidelines, which you may wish to adapt to your situation, are the following:

a. Anything said in this group is considered confidential and will not be discussed outside the group unless specific permission is given to do so.

b. We will provide time for each person present to talk if he or she feels comfortable doing so.

c. We will talk about ourselves and our own situations, avoiding conversation about other people.

d. We will listen attentively to each other.

e. We will pray for each other.

7. Enjoy your study. Prepare to grow. God bless.

Suggestions for Group Leaders

There are specific suggestions to help you in leading in the guidelines for leaders and in the study notes at the back of this guide. Read the guidelines for leaders carefully, even if you are only leading one group meeting. Then you can go to the section on the particular session you will lead.

Introduction: Have You Ever Felt Like a Spiritual Failure?

I grew up feeling like a spiritual failure. When I was a teenager, we often had altar calls on Sunday nights at church, which provided an opportunity for people to make a commitment to Jesus Christ. Time after time, my friends and I would go forward.

We knew we were already saved, but somehow we still felt like failures. We were unable to keep all of the rules handed down to us. I remember the continual sense of condemnation. I was just never quite good enough. Yet my friends and I didn't want to go back to the world's way of doing things—we were stranded in no man's land! Why do so many of us, clinging to our faith, struggle on year after year but never seem to enjoy the victorious Christian life?

Since those early days as a Christian, I have discovered some biblical keys for experiencing this joy. These are keys that have liberated my personal walk with the Lord, and have brought freedom and release to many I have been privileged to talk with. They are simple things, but sometimes the simplest things are the most profound.

You'll find many of those keys in these studies as you discover how we can actively bring every aspect of our lives into God's will.

Knowing God's will involves much more than making a series of decisions that God would approve of. It means committing our entire lives to him as our sovereign Lord.

Perhaps you feel you are not a "good" Christian. Perhaps you wonder how you could tell others of the grace of Jesus when you fail to experience that grace so often. Perhaps there is one sin that has defeated you for a long time. Regardless of your situation, God's Word promises victory. We can live in a close relationship with him.

Our attitude toward Jesus may sometimes be hardhearted or half-hearted. But with the power of his grace, our commitment to him can in fact be wholehearted.

For further reading: the introduction, "Have You Ever Felt Like a Failure?" in Basic Discipleship. *(This guide builds on ideas outlined in* Basic Discipleship. *Recommended reading at the end of each study points you to the appropriate section of that book.)*

Study One
Lord of All

1 John 1

J esus must be Lord of all of my life or he cannot be Lord at all. My *whole* life must be his. That does not mean that I must be perfect to accept Jesus Christ as my Savior. It does not mean that I must live the rest of my life sinlessly or that I won't struggle to give some things up to the Lord.

Most of us, for example, are emotionally attached to things such as food, friends, job or lifestyle. These give us feelings of security, identity and meaning. But as the Holy Spirit slowly penetrates our hearts, we realize our identity and security must be in the Lord.

You might say, "Well, I'm doing pretty good. I have given most of those areas to the Lord, I am holding back on just one or two." I don't want to shock you, but that is not enough. Jesus does not want 51 percent or even 98 percent control of our lives. He wants to be in control of all areas.

Open

☐ What recent decisions have you made in which you actively sought the Lord's guidance?

☐ In what parts of life do you hesitate to give God control?

  __ family   __ social

  __ recreational   __ work

  __ spiritual   __ other: _____

☐ Why do you think you feel this reluctance?

__ The Lord might ask me   __ I have ambitions and
     to do more than I'm willing   plans I want to fulfill.
     to do.

__ I like my current comfort   __ other: _____
     level.

Study

Read 1 John 1:

¹That which was from the beginning, which we have heard, which we have seen with our eyes, which we have looked at and our hands have touched—this we proclaim concerning the Word of life. ²The life appeared; we have seen it and testify to it, and we proclaim to you the eternal life, which was with the Father and has appeared to us. ³We proclaim to you what we have seen and heard, so that you also may have fellowship with us. And our fellowship is with the Father and with his Son, Jesus Christ. ⁴We write this to make our joy complete.

⁵This is the message we have heard from him and declare to you: God is light; in him there is no darkness at all. ⁶If we claim to have fellowship with him yet walk in the darkness, we lie and do not live by the truth. ⁷But if we walk in the light, as he is in the light, we have fellowship with one another, and the blood of Jesus, his Son, purifies us from all sin.

⁸If we claim to be without sin, we deceive ourselves and the truth is not in us. ⁹If we confess our sins, he is faithful and just and will forgive us our sins and purify us from all unrighteousness. ¹⁰If we claim we have not sinned, we make him out to be a liar and his word has no place in our lives.

1. The apostle John is looking back to his early experience as a follower of Jesus. To what is he referring in the first three verses?

2. Why is John eager to proclaim this "life" to his readers (vv. 3-4)?

3. In verses 5-10 what contrasts are drawn?

Why do you think John drew attention to these contrasts?

4. What is Jesus able to do for us (vv. 7, 9)?

5. How does refusal to confess sin affect the lordship of Christ over a believer's life (vv. 6, 8, 10)?

6. When have you come out of darkness into God's light and found forgiveness?

Commit

☐ The relationship we have with the Lord should be dynamic and growing. His lordship must be ever expanding and increasing over each new stage of our lives. Where are you still choosing to "walk in darkness"—that is, hold something back from Christ's control?

☐ What are some changes you are willing to make in order to come into the full light of Christ?

Acknowledge that Jesus is Lord, and thank him for being your Savior. Surrender to him those parts of your life where you have preferred to keep control.

For further reading: chapter one of Basic Discipleship.

Study Two
The Framework of Obedience

Galatians 5:16-26

O nce we give our lives to God, the first question is often "What does he want me to do with my life?" Many Christians focus this question on issues of career and marriage. But God has much more in mind than this. And what he has in mind is not hard to discover.

Scripture reveals certain principles and truths that are God's will for us regardless of our personal situations and circumstances. Before God can use us or give us "special assignments," he has to know if we can be trusted with what he has already given us. To know God's will for the future, we must first obey what we already know in the present!

Open

☐ Why are you interested in knowing God's will?

☐ What do you think of the statement "To know God's will for the future, we must first obey what we already know in the present"? Explain why you do or don't agree.

Study

Read Galatians 5:16-26:

[16]So I say, live by the Spirit, and you will not gratify the desires of the sinful nature. [17]For the sinful nature desires what is contrary to the Spirit, and the Spirit what is contrary to the sinful nature. They are in conflict with each other, so that you do not do what you want. [18]But if you are led by the Spirit, you are not under law.

[19]The acts of the sinful nature are obvious: sexual immorality, impurity and debauchery; [20]idolatry and witchcraft; hatred, discord, jealousy, fits of rage, selfish ambition, dissensions, factions [21]and envy; drunkenness, orgies, and the like. I warn you, as I did before, that those who live like this will not inherit the kingdom of God.

[22]But the fruit of the Spirit is love, joy, peace, patience, kind-

ness, goodness, faithfulness, [23]gentleness and self-control. Against such things there is no law. [24]Those who belong to Christ Jesus have crucified the sinful nature with its passions and desires. [25]Since we live by the Spirit, let us keep in step with the Spirit. [26]Let us not become conceited, provoking and envying each other.

1. Two qualities of life are contrasted in this passage. How would you characterize each?

2. What will help guard us against sin (vv. 16-17)?

3. As you consider the list of sins in verses 19-21, which ones do you see as prevalent in our society?

Which ones do you see as prevalent in yourself?

4. This is a very ugly list of sins. Why would such behavior appeal to anyone?

5. The qualities in verses 22-23 are called "the fruit of the Spirit." How do these qualities reflect the Lord Jesus Christ living in a person?

6. When have you seen one or more of the fruit of the Spirit in your life as a result of your obedience to the Lord?

Commit ————————————————————————
☐ Complete this statement: I would like to obey the Lord _____

_____

_____.

(More fully, more joyfully, more consistently, more courageously, more selflessly and so on.)

☐ Pick one fruit of the Spirit that you long to see increasing in your life, and make a specific plan to pray regularly and obey the Lord in this area.

Think of specific situations where you can obey Christ to a deeper and more radical extent. Rely on his strength, not your own.

For further reading: chapter two of Basic Discipleship.

Study Three
Being Faithful

Matthew 25:31-46

A pastor in the Midwest relayed the following problem to one of our mission leaders:

> We have a young couple who came home from serving God overseas to raise financial support. They asked if the church would consider supporting them, and in return they would commit themselves to the church for one year. We agreed to this arrangement. But, for the six months they've been with us we only see them once a week—Sunday mornings. They don't offer to take Sunday school, take turns cleaning or help with the youth group. If that's their idea of serving, then we feel used and don't think they have what it takes to be a missionary. We don't want to support them because they're not worth sending out as missionaries with your organization.

When I heard of the situation, I thought: "The pastor is right. This couple does not deserve to be supported or to be full-time mission-

aries. They haven't been responsible. They haven't shown humility
and proved themselves in the local church."

If we cannot serve God in the situation we're in right now, then
what makes us think we can do better in a different location or
position? The human tendency is to avoid the mundane and
graduate to the spectacular, but that is not God's way. Godly
character exemplified through the fruit of the Spirit can be as
easily seen in small tasks as in large ones.

Open

☐ What kind of ministry do you think God has called you to?

☐ What kinds of responsibilities do you have now?

☐ How can faithfulness now in these responsibilities prepare you
for ministry in the future?

Study

Read Matthew 25:31-46:

³¹When the Son of Man comes in his glory, and all the angels
with him, he will sit on his throne in heavenly glory. ³²All the nations
will be gathered before him, and he will separate the people one from
another as a shepherd separates the sheep from the goats. ³³He will
put the sheep on his right and the goats on his left.

[34] Then the King will say to those on his right, "Come, you who are blessed by my Father; take your inheritance, the kingdom prepared for you since the creation of the world. [35]For I was hungry and you gave me something to eat, I was thirsty and you gave me something to drink, I was a stranger and you invited me in, [36]I needed clothes and you clothed me, I was sick and you looked after me, I was in prison and you came to visit me."

[37]Then the righteous will answer him, "Lord, when did we see you hungry and feed you, or thirsty and give you something to drink? [38]When did we see you a stranger and invite you in, or needing clothes and clothe you? [39]When did we see you sick or in prison and go to visit you?"

[40]The King will reply, "I tell you the truth, whatever you did for one of the least of these brothers of mine, you did for me."

[41]Then he will say to those on his left, "Depart from me, you who are cursed, into the eternal fire prepared for the devil and his angels. [42]For I was hungry and you gave me nothing to eat, I was thirsty and you gave me nothing to drink, [43]I was a stranger and you did not invite me in, I needed clothes and you did not clothe me, I was sick and in prison and you did not look after me."

[44]They also will answer, "Lord, when did we see you hungry or thirsty or a stranger or needing clothes or sick or in prison, and did not help you?"

[45]He will reply, "I tell you the truth, whatever you did not do for one of the least of these, you did not do for me."

[46]Then they will go away to eternal punishment, but the righteous to eternal life.

---

1. Picture the dramatic scene Jesus draws. What do you imagine are the reactions on the faces of both the "sheep" and the "goats"?

2. Why do you think both the sheep and the goats are surprised by the King's words (vv. 34-36, 41-43)?

3. What had the sheep done without realizing it (vv. 37-40)?

4. What are some small ways that you can serve those you come into contact with each day?

5. If we consistently fail to do small jobs well, what might that say about our character?

6. What had the goats failed to recognize as they went about their everyday lives (vv. 41-45)?

7. Why do we overlook or ignore people in need?

8. What difference will it make in the mundane details of life if we realize we're doing them to and for Christ?

Commit

☐ Where do you tend to slack off and not fulfill your responsibilities faithfully?

☐ How can you serve the Lord in some ordinary job which seems insignificant?

☐ Often we can't move right away into the ministry to which we believe God is calling us. What practical steps can you take now to prepare for when God shows you the time is right?

Pray that you will see Jesus in the faces of ordinary people and that you will serve him as you serve them.

For further reading: chapter three of Basic Discipleship.

Study Four
Be All God Wants You to Be
Ephesians 1:1-14

*T*here are some Christians who have what I call "the martyr complex." These folks automatically assume God is going to force them to do the very thing they hate most. If they like warm weather, God will obviously call them to Alaska, or if they like working with gadgets and machines, they're destined to spend the rest of their lives on a remote Pacific island where there are no electric sockets.

We must be very careful with this kind of attitude lest we misrepresent God's character and portray him as a gigantic killjoy. There may be times when God requires us to do something we do not enjoy and would not naturally choose, but since God created us to be the kind of people we are, he pays careful attention to our personalities and natural gifts when he gives us special assignments.

What are our spiritual gifts? And what special assignment does God have for us?

Open

☐ When you think of your God-given abilities and gifts, how do you respond?

__ I have a good idea what they are.

__ I wish I knew what they are.

__ I'm not positive what they are.

__ I'm glad for the abilities God has given me.

__ I once thought I knew what my gifts were, but circumstances didn't bear it out.

__ Sometimes I'm jealous of the abilities God has given others.

☐ How have you benefited from other people's spiritual gifts?

Study

Read Ephesians 1:1-14:

[1]Paul, an apostle of Christ Jesus by the will of God,

To the saints in Ephesus, the faithful in Christ Jesus:

[2]Grace and peace to you from God our Father and the Lord Jesus Christ.

[3]Praise be to the God and Father of our Lord Jesus Christ, who has blessed us in the heavenly realms with every spiritual blessing in Christ. [4]For he chose us in him before the creation of the world to be holy and blameless in his sight. In love [5]he predestined us to be adopted as his sons through Jesus Christ, in accordance with his pleasure and will—[6]to the praise of his glorious grace, which he has freely given us in the One he loves. [7]In him we have redemption through his blood, the forgiveness of sins, in accor-

dance with the riches of God's grace [8] that he lavished on us with all wisdom and understanding. [9] And he made known to us the mystery of his will according to his good pleasure, which he purposed in Christ, [10] to be put into effect when the times will have reached their fulfillment—to bring all things in heaven and on earth together under one head, even Christ.

[11] In him we were also chosen, having been predestined according to the plan of him who works out everything in conformity with the purpose of his will, [12] in order that we, who were the first to hope in Christ, might be for the praise of his glory. [13] And you also were included in Christ when you heard the word of truth, the gospel of your salvation. Having believed, you were marked in him with a seal, the promised Holy Spirit, [14] who is a deposit guaranteeing our inheritance until the redemption of those who are God's possession—to the praise of his glory.

---

1. Taking this passage as a whole, how would you describe God's disposition toward humanity?

---

2. This Scripture assures us that God has blessed us with "every spiritual blessing in Christ" (v. 3), but it also mentions specific blessings. What are those blessings?

3. How are your natural gifts and abilities blessings from God in your life?

in the lives of others?

4. What kinds of responses have you received from others which help you identify your gifts and abilities?

5. What does this passage tell you about how God regards you as an individual?

6. Consider: The Lord has chosen us and has given us wisdom and understanding to know his will and to live for the praise of his glory (vv. 4, 8-9, 11-12). How can you apply these truths to your spiritual gifts?

Commit

☐ Complete this statement: "I believe God has given me the ability to _____. "

☐ How will others lose out if you do not use your gifts and abilities for the glory of God?

☐ If you are not sure what your gifts are, how will you go about exploring for them?

Thank the Lord for giving you spiritual blessings in Christ, enabling you to live for him. Pray for wisdom to know your gifts and the courage to let God put them to use.

For further reading: chapters four and five of Basic Discipleship.

Study Five
Whom Do We Serve?

Romans 6:12-23

I magine that I wrote Sally (my wife) asking her to marry me, and her response was something like this:

Dear Floyd,

I would love to marry you. It's a dream come true. Thank you. There are a few minor details, though.

I have a couple of other boyfriends—well, ten to be exact. Most of them don't mean much to me, but can I keep Fred and Dennis? I must be in love, because I've never before been willing to give up so many of my boyfriends! Mom says you're a lucky man!

There's one other thing. I will accept your proposal on the condition that I can stay in Texas and live with my parents. I love them. They have done so much for me that I couldn't dream of leaving them. You wouldn't want me to hurt their feelings, would you? However, you can visit whenever you want. I'm sure you'll understand.

I look forward to setting the wedding date!

Yours in undying love and devotion,

Sally

If I had received that kind of reply from Sally to my marriage proposal, I would not have married her. I don't think any of us would! When I asked Sally to marry me, I expected that she would lay aside all others for me, and I would do likewise. That is what marriage is about—committing ourselves wholeheartedly to the other person. We would feel cheated if our partner suggested any other kind of relationship.

How then does God feel when we say, "Lord, I love you so much that I'm going to give up everything in my life except John"—or Kathy or my stereo or my car or my job or whatever else is important? Or we say, "I want to serve you, but please don't send me to the mission field. I couldn't do that to my family!"

Open

☐ Who do you spend the most time and energy serving?

__ my boss   __ my family   __ myself

— my customers   __ my church   __ the Lord

__ the Lord through one or more of the above

__ someone or something else:_____

☐ What competes with the Lord for your loyalty?

Study

Read Romans 6:12-23:

[12]Therefore do not let sin reign in your mortal body so that you obey its evil desires. [13]Do not offer the parts of your body to sin, as instruments of wickedness, but rather offer yourselves to God, as those who have been brought from death to life; and offer the parts of your body to him as instruments of righteousness. [14]For sin shall not be your master, because you are not under law, but under grace.

[15]What then? Shall we sin because we are not under law but under grace? By no means! [16]Don't you know that when you offer yourselves to someone to obey him as slaves, you are slaves to the one whom you obey—whether you are slaves to sin, which leads to death, or to obedience, which leads to righteousness? [17]But thanks be to God that, though you used to be slaves to sin, you wholeheartedly obeyed the form of teaching to which you were entrusted. [18]You have been set free from sin and have become slaves to righteousness.

[19]I put this in human terms because you are weak in your natural selves. Just as you used to offer the parts of your body in slavery to impurity and to ever-increasing wickedness, so now offer them in slavery to righteousness leading to holiness. [20]When you were slaves to sin, you were free from the control of righteousness. [21]What benefit did you reap at that time from the things you are now ashamed of? Those things result in death! [22]But now that you have been set free from sin and have become slaves to God, the benefit you reap leads to holiness, and the result is eternal life. [23]For the wages of sin is death, but the gift of God is eternal life in Christ Jesus our Lord.

1. What choices does this Scripture present to believers? (Note

specifically verses 13, 16 and 19.)

2. Three times death is named as the result of yielding to sin (vv. 16, 21, 23). What sort(s) of death do you think Paul refers to?

3. What are other results of being a slave to sin (vv. 19, 21)?

4. How is sin overcome (vv. 12-14, 22-23)?

5. Humanly speaking, a released slave is a free person. Paul says here that a person freed from slavery to sin becomes a new kind of slave (v. 16). How would you contrast this new type of slavery with the old?

6. How does Paul answer the suggestion that a believer can go ahead and sin freely because grace will cover the sin (vv. 15-18)?

Commit

☐ Today many people work as contract workers, taking on only those jobs they choose for a limited period of time. Contract work is in sharp contrast to the work of a slave, who serves the master unconditionally, with no options for other kinds of service. Which form of service best describes your relationship with God? Why?

☐ What decisions and actions will it take for you to genuinely become the slave of the Lord?

Surrender your life to Christ more fully than ever. Resolve to follow his orders unconditionally.

For further reading: chapter six of Basic Discipleship.

Study Six
Open to God
1 Corinthians 10:1-13

I magine that the angel Gabriel is sent to you with a special "moral Polaroid camera." This camera can take pictures of your thought life when there is unconfessed sin. These photographs can then be developed and sold through mail order or at the front of your church for twenty-five cents apiece.

How would you feel about the above scenario? Are you happy for people to know your secret thoughts?

Jesus is Lord. So where do I start living under his lordship? John wrote, "If we walk in the light, as he is in the light, we have fellowship with one another, and the blood of Jesus, his Son, purifies us from all sin" (1 John 1:7). We sing about walking in the light. The phrase adorns posters, napkin holders and T-shirts. Yet despite its usage in popular Christian culture, I wonder if many of us really know what is meant by "walking in the light."

The phrase has a very spiritual sound to it, but it is also very down-to-earth. It means living in a state of honesty, with desires of our hearts known to both God and others.

Open

☐ Think of an area in which you often face temptation to sin. How do you usually respond?

__ I make an excuse for giving in.

__ I resist, though I don't enjoy it.

__ I am not very aware of temptation.

__ I consciously bring it to the Lord.

__ I deny the fact that I'm being tempted.

__ I get worried that my spiritual life is not what it should be.

☐ What do you find easy to be honest about with God?

☐ What do you find hardest to be honest about with God?

Study

Read 1 Corinthians 10:1-13:

[1]For I do not want you to be ignorant of the fact, brothers, that our forefathers were all under the cloud and that they all passed through the sea. [2]They were all baptized into Moses in the cloud and in the sea. [3]They all ate the same spiritual food [4]and drank the same spiritual drink; for they drank from the spiritual rock that accompanied them, and that rock was Christ. [5]Nevertheless,

God was not pleased with most of them; their bodies were scattered over the desert.

⁶Now these things occurred as examples to keep us from setting our hearts on evil things as they did. ⁷Do not be idolaters, as some of them were; as it is written: "The people sat down to eat and drink and got up to indulge in pagan revelry." ⁸We should not commit sexual immorality, as some of them did—and in one day twenty-three thousand of them died. ⁹We should not test the Lord, as some of them did—and were killed by snakes. ¹⁰And do not grumble, as some of them did—and were killed by the destroying angel.

¹¹These things happened to them as examples and were written down as warnings for us, on whom the fulfillment of the ages has come. ¹²So, if you think you are standing firm, be careful that you don't fall! ¹³No temptation has seized you except what is common to man. And God is faithful; he will not let you be tempted beyond what you can bear. But when you are tempted, he will also provide a way out so that you can stand up under it.

---

1. This passage opens with references to the experiences of the Israelites after they left Egypt in the exodus. What advantages did they enjoy (vv. 1-4)?

---

2. Despite all the advantages God gave them, what sins did they fall into (vv. 5-10)?

---

3. How can the Israelites in the desert serve as examples (although bad examples) for us (vv. 6, 11)?

4. How does verse 12 speak to you in the areas where you feel strongest spiritually?

5. In every temptation we face, what assurances does the Lord give us (v. 13)?

6. When and how have you seen God graciously provide the escape mentioned in verse 13?

Commit ————————————————————————

☐ We need to come into the presence of a holy God and say: "God, here are my thoughts. They are ugly and impure, and I need your help. I don't want them." When we do this with each and every sinful thought, we allow Jesus to break into our lives and bring his help and light into the struggle. What desires, resentments or other trouble-some thoughts do you need to bring to the light of Jesus?

☐ Where and when do you especially need to stay open to God?

Open yourself to the purifying power of the Holy Spirit. Confess any sin that has been hidden, and accept the mercy of Jesus' death and resurrection for you. Praise God that he is with you in all that you do.

For further reading: chapter seven of Basic Discipleship.

Guidelines for Leaders

Leading a Bible discussion can be an enjoyable and rewarding experience. But it can also be intimidating—especially if you've never done it before. If this is how you feel, you're in good company.

Remember when God asked Moses to lead the Israelites out of Egypt? Moses replied, "O Lord, please send someone else to do it" (Exodus 4:13). But God gave Moses the help (human and divine) he needed to be a strong leader.

Leading a Bible discussion is not difficult if you follow certain guidelines. You don't need to be an expert on the Bible or a trained teacher. The suggestions listed below can help you to effectively fulfill your role as leader—and enjoy doing it.

Preparing for the Study

1. As you study the passage ahead of time, ask God to help you understand it and apply it in your own life. Unless this happens, you will not be prepared to lead others. Pray too for the various members

of the group. Ask God to open your hearts to the message of his Word and motivate you to action.

2. Read the introduction to the entire guide to get an overview of the subject at hand and the issues which will be explored.

3. Be ready for the "Open" questions with a personal story or example. The group will be only as vulnerable and open as its leader.

4. As you begin preparing for each study, read and reread the assigned Bible passage to familiarize yourself with it. You may want to look up the passage in a Bible so that you can see its context.

5. This study guide is based on the New International Version of the Bible. That is what is reproduced in your guide. It will help you and the group if you use this translation as the basis for your study and discussion.

6. Carefully work through each question in the study. Spend time in meditation and reflection as you consider how to respond.

7. Write your thoughts and responses in the space provided in the study guide. This will help you to express your understanding of the passage clearly.

8. It might help you to have a Bible dictionary handy. Use it to look up any unfamiliar words, names or places. (For additional help on how to study a passage, see chapter five of *Leading Bible Discussions*, IVP.)

9. Take the final (application) questions and the "Commit" portion of each study seriously. Consider what this means for your life, what changes you may need to make in your lifestyle and/or what actions you can take in your church or with people you know. Remember that the group will follow your lead in responding to the studies.

Leading the Study

1. Be sure everyone in your group has a study guide and Bible. Encourage the group to prepare beforehand for each discussion by reading the introduction to the guide and by working through the questions in the study.

2. At the beginning of your first time together, explain that these studies are meant to be discussions, not lectures. Encourage the members of the group to participate. However, do not put pressure on those who may be hesitant to speak during the first few sessions.

3. Begin the study on time. Open with prayer, asking God to help the group understand and apply the passage.

4. Have a group member read the introductory paragraph at the beginning of the discussion. This will remind the group of the topic of the study.

5. Every study begins with a section called *Open*. These "approach" questions are meant to be asked before the passage is read. They are important for several reasons.

First, there is always a stiffness that needs to be overcome before people will begin to talk openly. A good question will break the ice.

Second, most people will have lots of different things going on in their minds (dinner, an exam, an important meeting coming up, how to get the car fixed) that have nothing to do with the study. A creative question will get their attention and draw them into the discussion.

Third, approach questions can reveal where our thoughts or feelings need to be transformed by Scripture. That is why it is especially important not to read the passage before the approach question is asked. The passage will tend to color the honest reactions people would otherwise give, because they feel they are supposed to think the way the Bible does.

6. Have a group member read aloud the passage to be studied.

7. As you ask the questions, keep in mind that they are designed to be used just as they are written. You may simply read them aloud. Or you may prefer to express them in your own words.

There may be times when it is appropriate to deviate from the study guide. For example, a question may already have been answered. If so, move on to the next question. Or someone may raise an important question not covered in the guide. Take time to discuss it, but try to keep the group from going off on tangents.

8. Avoid answering your own questions. Repeat or rephrase them if necessary until they are clearly understood. An eager group quickly becomes passive and silent if members think the leader will give all the *right* answers.

9. Don't be afraid of silence. People may need time to think about the question before formulating their answers.

10. Don't be content with just one answer. Ask, "What do the rest of you think?" or, "Anything else?" until several people have given answers to a question.

11. Acknowledge all contributions. Be affirming whenever possible. Never reject an answer. If it is clearly off-base, ask, "Which verse led you to that conclusion?" or, "What do the rest of you think?"

12. Don't expect every answer to be addressed to you, even though this will probably happen at first. As group members become more at ease, they will begin to truly interact with each other. This is one sign of healthy discussion.

13. Don't be afraid of controversy. It can be stimulating! If you don't resolve an issue completely, don't be frustrated. Move on and keep it in mind for later. A subsequent study may solve the problem.

14. Periodically summarize what the group has said about the passage. This helps to draw together the various ideas mentioned and gives continuity to the study. But don't preach.

15. Don't skip over the application questions at the end of each study. It's important that we each apply the message of the passage to ourselves in a specific way. Be willing to get things started by describing how you have been affected by the study.

Depending on the makeup of your group and the length of time you've been together, you may or may not want to discuss the "Commit" section. If not, allow the group to read it and reflect on it silently. Encourage members to make specific commitments and to write them in their study guide. Ask them the following week how they did with their commitments.

16. Conclude your time together with conversational prayer. Ask for God's help in following through on the commitments you've made.

17. End on time.

Many more suggestions and helps are found in *The Big Book on Small Groups, Small Group Leaders' Handbook* and *Good Things Come in Small Groups* (IVP). Reading through one of these books would be worth your time.

Study Notes

Study One. Lord of All. 1 John 1.

Purpose: To be challenged to allow Christ to be Lord of our entire lives.

Question 1. "That which was from the beginning, which we have heard, which we have seen with our eyes, which we have looked at and our hands have touched . . . the Word of life" (v. 1) can only refer to the Lord Jesus Christ in the flesh, as John first knew him.

Question 3. Note the contrasts between light and darkness—finding the light with God, who has not darkness, walking in light versus walking in darkness, truth and falsehood, and claiming sinlessness and confessing sin.

Question 4. The greatest motivation to victory in the Christian life is the assurance that Jesus is within us and his grace is greater than any temptation we will ever face. He is more committed to our victory over sin than we are!

Question 5. Some professing Christians want all the blessings of being a Christian—such as forgiveness, healing, hope and eternal life—but they do not want to pay the price of dying to their own will and letting Jesus rule over them. Jesus does not want to break our will, but he will cross it. We must put his will above ours. In that process we must die to ourselves in the sense that we will not insist on living for what we want first, but put his character and his desires above our own.

Question 6. Think not only of when you first trusted Christ for salvation, but also of other times since then, when you confessed sin and knew his forgiveness.

Study Two. The Framework of Obedience. Galatians 5:16-26.
Purpose: To deepen our commitment to obeying Christ.

Question 1. In life, we must choose to go in one of two directions. One is the way of human lusts. The other is doing the will of God. At one end of the scale we go our own way and enjoy what we consider to be the pleasures of life. At the other end, we submit to the will of God and live our lives to please him. It is God's will that we follow his Spirit rather than our selfish desires.

Question 2. In Romans 8:5-6 Paul elaborated on living by the Holy Spirit: "Those who live according to the sinful nature have their minds set on what that nature desires; but those who live in accordance with the Spirit have their minds set on what the Spirit desires. The mind of sinful man is death, but the mind controlled by the Spirit is life and peace."

In some Bible translations the word *flesh* appears in Galatians 5:16, 17, 19 and 24, and Romans 8:5. Here it means not the physical body but sinful human nature, which wars against the Holy Spirit and which the Holy Spirit seeks to overcome.

Question 4. As you go through the list, notice which ones fit in the categories of either selfish pleasure or personal power.

Question 5. In his life on earth, Jesus flawlessly exhibited all these

traits. By his Spirit he lives within believers, as he promised in John
14:15-20.

Study Three. Being Faithful. Matthew 25:31-46.
Purpose: To accept service in small things as preparation for larger
responsibilities.
Open. This does not refer to a call to full-time professional ministry.
We are all called to ministry in the church, in our neighborhoods, at
work and so on.
Question 1. "Although sheep and goats grazed together, it is said
that Palestinian shepherds normally separated sheep and goats at
night because goats need to be warm at night while sheep prefer open
air. Sheep were more valuable than goats, and characteristics like
this may have influenced how these terms would be heard figura-
tively" (Craig S. Keener, *The IVP Bible Background Commentary:
New Testament* [Downers Grove, Ill.: InterVarsity Press, 1993], p.
118).
Question 3. "Jesus looked for people who would not merely do good
but be good, who enjoy goodness and for whom goodness is its own
reward. . . . The reward for good conduct is the invitation 'enter into
the joy of your Lord.' The ultimate reward is being the kind of person
who can enjoy God. The true end of human beings is to glorify God
and enjoy him forever, an idea which would then raise for Jesus'
hearers a question: are they the sort of people who would enjoy
God?" (L. D. Hurst, "Ethics of Jesus," in *Dictionary of Jesus and
the Gospels*, ed. Joel B. Green, Scot McKnight and I. Howard
Marshall [Downers Grove, Ill.: InterVarsity Press, 1992], p. 215).
Question 5. If we neglect to serve God in small things, we are not yet
ready to serve him in larger things. Throughout the Bible, God gives
people promises of the great things he wants to do through them, but

seldom are the promises fulfilled immediately. There are often aspects of people's character that have to be worked out before they are ready to handle the ministry or opportunity God has for them. God wants to develop in us the character strengths of stability, consistency and responsibility.

Study Four. Be All God Wants You to Be. Ephesians 1:1-14.
Purpose: To put to use the special abilities God has given us.

Question 2. God has chosen us (vv. 4, 11), made us holy and blameless in his sight (v. 4), adopted us as his children (v. 5), given us his grace freely (v. 6), redeemed and forgiven us (v. 7), given us wisdom and understanding (v. 8), revealed his will to us (v. 9), and sealed us with the Holy Spirit as a guarantee of our inheritance (vv. 13-14).

Question 4. The people God places around us are like mirrors. They reflect back to us, through their comments and insights, what our gifts and strengths are. While we should never be governed solely by another person's opinion of us, others can prove valuable in assessing our strengths and weaknesses. Listen to what other people have to say about you, both the positive and the negative. What do you receive the most compliments for? What do people see in you that you have not seen in yourself?

Questions 5-6. When evaluating themselves, people tend to swing toward one of two extremes. They either underestimate or overestimate their abilities, and both are debilitating. We are admonished in Scripture not to think more highly of ourselves than we ought, but to think of ourselves with sober judgment (Romans 12:3). There are many Christians sitting in pews doing nothing because they feel they haven't been offered a position worthy of them. Conversely, many people are waiting in the wings until they feel more worthy or until they have something spiritual to offer. Spiritual gifts and natural abilities are both discovered and developed by stepping out and doing something that needs to be done. For further study of spiritual gifts, you may wish to study Ephesians 4:1-16; 1 Corinthians and Romans 12:1-8.

Study Five. Whom Do We Serve? Romans 6:12-23.

Purpose: To forsake sin and submit to Christ as master.

Question 1. The basic choice, repeated several times, is that of offering ourselves either to sin or to righteousness. There is no third alternative of being neutral.

Question 2. The original sin of humanity led to universal physical death; but Paul must mean something beyond the fact that all people die, since the death he refers to is one we can escape by yielding to righteousness. Sin can lead to an individual sinner's death—for example, drugging oneself to death or committing a capital offense. More generally, sin leads to spiritual death, which is separation from God, in contrast to eternal life with God (vv. 22-23).

Question 5. The slave of righteousness recognizes Christ as master. The believer yields everything to the Lord (vv. 13, 19), becomes holy (vv. 19, 22) and gains eternal life (vv. 22-23). In Jewish law, a freed Hebrew slave could declare that he wanted to remain with his master. His ear would be pierced as a sign of his decision.

Study Six. Open to God. 1 Corinthians 10:1-13.

Purpose: To take the escape routes from temptation which God mercifully provides.

Question 1. After they were miraculously freed from slavery in Egypt, the Israelites were led each day by a cloud (Exodus 13:21-22) and escaped through the Red Sea (Exodus 14:21-29). During their desert travels, the Lord provided food and water (Exodus 16—17).

Question 2. The incidents mentioned are found in Exodus 32; Numbers 25, 21 and 16.

Question 3. There is a tendency for those who have been Christians for some time or who hold positions of spiritual leadership to convey the impression that they are beyond temptation. This is a dangerous situation, both for those who think it and for the younger Christians who may believe them. All of us, regardless of our years or position, are going to face temptation and struggle in our lives.

Question 4. We are not to deliberately put ourselves in a place of temptation, either to prove how strong we are or because we are denying we have a weakness in a particular area of our lives. Christians must flee temptation, not flirt with it.

Question 5. Read the Old and New Testaments and you will find any number of sins and failures. But read too of the God who forgives, who picks us up and puts our feet on solid ground. He loves us, and for our ultimate good wants us to be honest before him by confessing our sins. If we humble ourselves, walk in the light and are willing to be known for who we really are, then he is willing and ready to help us.

Christian Basics Bible Studies from InterVarsity Press

Christian Basics are the keys to becoming a mature disciple. The studies in these guides, based on material from some well-loved books (which can be read along with the studies), will take you through key Scripture passages and help you to apply biblical truths to your life. Each guide has six studies for individuals or groups.

Certainty: Know Why You Believe by Paul Little with Scott Hotaling. Faith means facing hard questions. Is Jesus the only way to God? Why does God allow suffering and evil? These questions need solid answers. These studies will guide you to Scripture to find a reasonable response to the toughest challenges you face.

Character: Who You Are When No One's Looking by Bill Hybels with Dale and Sandy Larsen. Courage. Discipline. Vision. Endurance. Compassion. Self-sacrifice. The qualities covered in this Bible study guide provide a foundation for character. With this foundation and God's guidance, we can maintain character even when we face temptations and troubles.

Christ: Basic Christianity by John Stott with Scott Hotaling. God himself is seeking us through his Son, Jesus Christ. But who is this Jesus? These studies explore the person and character of the man who has altered the face of history. Discover him for the first time or in a new and deeper way.

Christ's Body: The Community of the King by Howard Snyder with Robbie and Breck Castleman. What is God's vision for the church? What is my role? What are my spiritual gifts? This guide helps illumine God's plan for the church and for each of us as a part of it.

Commitment: My Heart—Christ's Home by Robert Boyd Munger with Dale and Sandy Larsen. What would it be like to have Christ come into the home of our hearts? Moving from the living room to the study to the recreation room with him, we discover what he desires for us. These studies will take you through six rooms of your heart. You will be stretched and enriched by your personal meetings with Christ in each study.

Decisions: Finding God's Will by J. I. Packer with Dale and Sandy Larsen. Facing a big decision? From job changes to marriage to buying a house, this guide will give you the biblical grounding you need to discover what God has in store for you.

Excellence: Run with the Horses by Eugene Peterson with Scott Hotaling. Life is difficult. Daily we must choose whether to live cautiously or courageously. God calls us to live at our best, to pursue righteousness, to sustain a drive toward excellence. These studies on Jeremiah's pursuit of excellence with God's help will motivate and inspire you.

Lordship: Basic Discipleship by Floyd McClung with Dale and Sandy Larsen. Have you ever felt like a spiritual failure? Does the Christian life seem like a set of rules that are impossible to follow? This guide contains the biblical keys to true discipleship. By following them you'll be liberated to serve God in every aspect of your life.

Perseverance: A Long Obedience in the Same Direction by Eugene Peterson with Dale and Sandy Larsen. When the going gets tough, what does a Christian do? This world is no friend to grace. God has given us some resources, however. As we grow in character qualities like hope, patience, repentance and joy, we will grow in our ability to persevere. The biblical passages in these studies offer encouragement to continue in the path Christ has set forth for us.

Prayer: Too Busy Not to Pray by Bill Hybels with Dale and Sandy Larsen. There's so much going on—work, church, school, family, relationships: the list is never-ending. Someone always seems to need something from us. But time for God, time to pray, seems impossible to find. These studies are designed to help you slow down and listen to God so that you can respond to him.

Priorities: Tyranny of the Urgent by Charles Hummel. Have you ever wished for a thirty-hour day? Every week we leave a trail of unfinished tasks. Unanswered letters, unvisited friends and unread books haunt our waking moments. We desperately need relief. This guide is designed to help you put your life back in order by discovering what is *really* important. Find out what God's priorities are for you.

Scripture: God's Word for Contemporary Christians by John Stott with Scott Hotaling. What is the place of Scripture in our lives? We know it is important—God's Word to us—but how can it make a difference to us each day? In this guide John Stott will show you the power Scripture can have in your life. These studies will help you make the Bible your anchor to God in the face of the temptation and corruption that are all around.

Spiritual Warfare: The Fight by John White with Dale and Sandy Larsen. As a Christian, you are a sworn foe of the legions of hell. They will oppose you as you obey Christ. Life with Jesus can be an exhilarating and reassuring experience of triumph over evil forces. But the battle never ends. This guide will help you prepare for war.

Witnessing: How to Give Away Your Faith by Paul Little with Dale and Sandy Larsen. If you want to talk about Jesus, but you're not sure what to say—or how to say it—this Bible study guide is for you. It will deepen your understanding of the essentials of faith and strengthen your confidence as you talk with others.

Work: Serving God by What We Do by Ben Patterson with Dietrich Gruen. "I can serve God in church, but can I serve him on the job?" In the factory, in the office, in the home, on the road, on the farm—Ben Patterson says we can give glory to God wherever he calls us. Work, even what seems to us the most mundane, is what God created us for. He is our employer. These studies will show you how your work can become meaningful and satisfying.

Worship: Serving God with Our Praise by Ben Patterson with Dietrich Gruen. Our deepest need can be filled only as we come to our Creator in worship. This is the divine drama in which we are all invited to participate, not as observers but as performers. True worship will transform every part of our lives, and these studies will help you to understand and experience the glory of praising God.